THE
LUTHER
LEGACY

THE LUTHER LEGACY

An Introduction to Luther's
Life and Thought for Today

George Wolfgang Forell

AUGSBURG Publishing House • Minneapolis

THE LUTHER LEGACY

Contents

Introduction   7

1   The Setting of Luther's Life   *11*

2   Luther's Childhood and Youth   *17*

3   The Monk   *23*

4   The University Professor   *29*

5   The Indulgence Controversy   *34*

6   The Great Debates   *40*

7   1520   *46*

8   Worms and Wartburg   *52*

9   Conflict and Controversy   *58*

10   Word and Sacrament   *64*

11   Faith Active in Love   *70*

12   The Legacy   *75*

Introduction

There are many reasons why one might want to remember and discuss a Christian theologian who has managed to excite politicians, psychologists, playwrights, and even preachers five hundred years after his birth. Most theologians are barely noticed while they are among us, and completely forgotten once they are dead. What was it that made Luther such a lasting presence not only in the Christian world, but also in Western culture?

Some of the reasons that have been offered for the attention given to Luther in the 20th century are simply wrong. For example, it is said that he laid the groundwork for capitalism or nationalism. He did not understand the economic changes caused by the explorations of his age, which eventually (much later, to be sure) produced modern capitalism. A rudimentary form of venture capitalism had existed long before Luther, and had facilitated both the discoveries of the explorers and the sale of indulgences. Nationalism in the modern sense of the word came into existence centuries after Luther's death. There was no German state in Luther's time. The emperor, who was also the king of Spain, spoke broken German. His Spanish was not much better, and he preferred to speak French. Soldiers in the 16th century were not nationalistic freedom fighters, but more like professional football players or hired guns who fought for those employers who could afford their services.

Furthermore, Luther was not a forerunner of Hitler (who, unlike Karl Marx, was not even nominally "Lutheran"), or even an anti-Semite. He did express vicious and deplorable anti-Jewish sentiments, precisely because he took the Old Testament and its patriarchs and prophets seriously. He felt threatened in the very center of his theology by the rabbinic exegesis of the Hebrew Bible, and by the hopes of his Jewish contemporaries that his critique of the established church might lead to a reexamination of all Christian claims and thus presage the coming of the Messiah.

Thus it appears that some fashionable reasons to remember Luther are wrong. There are also others, which are, at best, dubious. The emphasis on Luther as a religious genius is beside the point, even if the various advocates of this view were more precise as to the exact meaning of the word "genius." Religious geniuses tend to be too idiosyncratic to be long remembered. Since their experience of the divine is so extraordinary, it cannot be replicated by ordinary people, and as a result they are soon forgotten. Like comets, they are spectacular to behold, but hardly a source of light or aids to navigation.

Not much more can be said in support of "Luther, the German Prophet." Most Germans are embarrassed by all the nonsense written on this topic. This title was indeed applied to him, even during his lifetime, but he observed, "this haughty title I will henceforth have to assign to myself, to please and oblige my papists and asses" (AE 47, 29), and promptly called himself something less pretentious, "a faithful teacher." Even if the years 1933-1945 could be blotted from memory, the description "German Prophet" tends to obscure our understanding of Luther. He was a German, but what makes him interesting today is the universal appeal of his understanding of the gospel. In fact, the somewhat surprising scope of the celebration of Luther's birthday by the government of the German Democratic Republic may be a combination of pride in their most famous native son (Marx, after all, was born in what is now the Federal Republic) and an understandable desire to attract western currency to their country from tourists interested in Luther's legacy. It is hardly "the German Prophet" who causes all this attention.

None of the significant sayings of Luther are limited

in their application to Germany. Even his frequent ex-coriation of German drunkenness might apply more generally than he thought. He did not translate the Bible into the German language because he thought German was more significant than other languages, but because the people he dealt with spoke it. The opinion that Luther's German Bible is superior to all other translations is a later development which, counter to Luther's commitment to the language of the people, retarded the acceptance of English as the language of the church of the Augsburg Confession in North America.

Thus, it is my claim that the reasons why one might want to recall Luther today are essentially theological—even if they have social and political implications. The brief chapters which follow are an effort to look at this theological legacy. But we should remember that Luther's theology was hammered out in the midst of life, a life of prayer and study, preaching, teaching, and debate. If we want to understand Luther, we must approach him not as archaeologists digging for the past, but as fellow Christians listening to a faithful teacher who tried to obey his Lord's command: "Go therefore and make disciples of all nations, baptizing them in the name of the Father and of the Son and of the Holy Spirit, teaching them to observe all that I have commanded you; and lo, I am with you always, to the close of the age" (Matt. 28:19-20).

Chapter 1

The Setting of Luther's Life

When the American astronauts set foot on the moon, the event was broadcast to the entire world, and people everywhere became instantaneously aware of it. Millions could actually see that first human step on the surface of the moon. Luther, born in Eisleben in what is today the German Democratic Republic, on Nov. 10, 1483, and baptized Martin on Nov. 11 (St. Martin's Day) in St. Peter's Church, was eight years old when Columbus and his crew set foot in the New World. While this event was to affect human history for centuries to come, and there would someday be millions of Christians who would be called "Lutherans" living in that New World, young Luther heard nothing about it. His access to the news was the town crier in Mansfeld, where the family had moved in 1484. His information concerning current events was limited to a more or less accurate version of the time of day and the events in Mansfeld and the immediate neighborhood.

What may be even more surprising to us, so fascinated by the national and international news, is that, even if Luther had heard about the "discovery of America," it would have meant little to him. Horizontal relationships from place to place or country to country, or even continent to continent, did not seem important to a man whose main interest was the vertical relationship between God and human beings. The only thing which ultimately mattered to Luther—and many of his contemporaries—was to get right with God. Explorations and scientific discoveries, even politics and economics, seemed petty by comparison. It is noteworthy that, while many people were willing to buy indulgences— tickets to heaven—few bought shares in the companies sponsoring the great explorations.

It was an age of extraordinary changes. Not many years before Luther's birth, Gutenberg had invented the printing press and durable movable type, thus introducing a new way of communicating information and ideas. Because of the printing press and its products, the world would be radically changed. Indeed, only decades later, Luther's writings would be spread with heretofore unimaginable rapidity across Europe, thanks to the printers' skill and greed (there were no author's royalties in those days). But in Mansfeld, young Luther knew nothing of this communications revolution.

The invention of the printing press and durable, movable type in the late 15th century radically changed the way ideas were communicated and allowed Luther's writings to spread swiftly throughout Europe.

In 1453, thirty years before Luther's birth, the Turks captured Constantinople by using formidable guns. The age of firearms and heavy artillery had begun, and it would change the world for centuries to come. Knights in armor became obsolete, for a bullet costing pennies could pierce armor costing thousands of dollars. City walls could be devastated by cannon, and castles like the Wartburg became useless from a military point of view. This revolution in military technology was neither known nor understood by Luther.

In 1513, a contemporary of Luther named Nicolo Machiavelli wrote a book called *The Prince,* in which he made a clear distinction between politics and morality, insisting that a successful prince or politician must always appear to be moral and pious, but in fact be unaffected by morality and piety in his own decisions. Machiavelli's ideal politician was Caesar Borgia, the son of Pope Alexander VI, known for his utter disdain for the conventional morality of his age. The ideas of Machiavelli (openly rejected, but secretly adopted by generations of kings and princes), which were to influence politics up to the present time, were unknown to Luther.

In the cities of Italy and southern Germany, a new way of doing business had been developed. One could make a great deal of money by investing in somewhat risky ventures, such as trade with the new world, or even through support of an ambitious church leader who needed money to increase his power by purchasing high ecclesiastical offices. While the Christian church had forbidden the purchase of ecclesiastical offices, describing it disdainfully as "simony," and had condemned the lending of money at interest as usury, it was now fashionable and profitable to make money by lending money. The Medici family in Italy and the Fuggers in Germany had accumulated vast fortunes in this manner. Luther became involved with both these prominent families, since Pope Leo X belonged to the Medici family, and the Fugger family had a stake in the indulgence sales. The bankers had offered one of their clients, the 23-year-old Albert of Hohenzollern, the means to repay the loans that he had obtained in order to acquire the offices of archbishop of Magdeburg, bishop of Halberstadt, and archbishop of Mainz. The sale of indulgences in the neighborhood of Wittenberg, which brought Luther into the fray, was sponsored by the Fugger banking house for this purpose. But Luther never understood capitalism, although he wrote eloquently against it, attacking the Fuggers by name in his *Address to the German Nobility* of 1520.

All in all, the setting of Luther's life was an age of radical change. While some of these changes had been under way for a long time, others were just beginning. Luther became involved in all of them willy-nilly. Yet he had a genuine concern that the church be an effective instrument of God's Word, and this also resulted in change. He was convinced that the church had become an unwieldy bureaucracy, a tool of human lust for power which served the ecclesiastical leadership and not the people they were called to serve. In an age of radical and pervasive change, Luther had a single-minded interest in what he called the "gospel," the good news of the forgiveness of sins for all human beings through the death and resurrection of Jesus Christ. Because he lived in the 16th century, Luther and his concern for the gospel became mixed up with all the other changes that were taking place everywhere. There was no way to keep these many movements neatly separated, even if Luther had had the benefit of our hindsight. We must understand Luther and his cause in the context of the time in which he lived, a time of radical change not unlike our own.

Chapter 2

Luther's Childhood and Youth

We know that Martin Luther was born on Nov. 10; his mother, Margaretta, remembered the date and the time distinctly. We are pretty sure that it was in 1483, the year he entered in the book when he matriculated at the University of Wittenberg. But friends and enemies soon argued about the year. It was an age which put much stock in astrology, though Luther himself considered it ridiculous. His friend Melanchthon, an addict of this pseudoscience, thought that Luther might have been born in 1484, which would have provided a better horoscope. An Italian mathematician, Jerome Cordanus, was sure that Luther was born on Oct. 22, 1483, at 10:00 P.M., since that time would, according to his astrological inquiries, have been the perfect moment for the birth of an archheretic.

Luther's father, Hans, worked in the copper mining industry in Mansfeld. This portrait was painted in 1527 by Lucas Cranach the Elder.

18

Even this trivial dispute illustrates how Luther's importance in the history of the church made every incident in his life the subject of controversy. While Luther liked to remind people that he descended from "real peasants," his father Hans no longer farmed, but had become a copper miner. He was an older son, and among the peasants in Thuringia, the youngest inherited the farm; the others had to make their own way without much parental help.

We don't know very much about his childhood. During Luther's early years, while his father was trying to get under way in the copper mining industry, young Martin felt that the family was quite poor, and he remembered that his mother had to carry her own firewood on her back from the woods surrounding Mansfeld.

Luther's earliest education was typical for the time. In the home, he learned to obey his parents, and corporal punishment was the order of the day. Late in life, he remembered that his mother had once caned him severely, " 'til I had bloody welts," because he had stolen a nut. His father whipped him, and so did his teachers in school, if he made the slightest mistake in his lessons. He was not yet five years old when he was taken to the local school, where he learned the "three Rs" and a little Latin. The importance of Latin for students at that time is hard to exaggerate. It was the international language of theology, law, medicine, and diplomacy. Competence in Latin made it possible to study or teach in Spain or England, Italy or France. All scholarly and scientific work was published in Latin. Without it, you were doomed to ignorance; with it, the world was open to you. Luther attended school in Mansfeld until 1497.

Of course, he went to church. In school, he had memorized the parts of the service: the Sanctus, the Benedictus, the Agnus Dei, and the Confiteor, all parts of the Mass. He also learned the Lord's Prayer, the Apostles' Creed, and the Ten Commandments. All these he used in church, along with short hymns in his own language celebrating Christmas, Easter, and Pentecost.

Besides the more formal lessons learned in home, church, and school, Luther picked up a great many of the popular superstitions of the age. He learned about elves, gnomes, and fairies, sprites, witches, and demons. The first edition of the notorious *Malleus Maleficarum*, the handbook for witch-hunters, had appeared four years after Luther's birth. Belief in witches was part of the conventional wisdom of the time, and Luther was never able to rid himself of such superstitions.

Shortly before his 14th birthday, he was sent away from home to continue his schooling in Magdeburg, one of the important cities of Germany at that time. The school he attended was run by the Brethren of the Common Life, a group of serious Christians belonging to a medieval revival movement specializing in the education of the young. Later, he remembered them as representatives of what was best in the church of his youth.

One other event which happened in Magdeburg he never seemed to be able to forget: he saw a real prince, William of Anhalt, who had left all the privileges of his station and had become a begging friar, emaciated and in tatters, walking with his beggar's sack through the streets of Magdeburg. "I saw him," he remembered, "carrying the sack like a donkey, looking like a skeleton, mere skin and bones. Nobody could see him without feeling ashamed of his own life." Luther stayed only a year in the big city, which probably proved too expensive for his parents. He continued his schooling in Eisenach, where his mother had relatives who were able to take an interest in the boy. This was probably not so easy for them, for, like other schoolboys at the time, he went from door to door singing for food and money. On one of these occasions, he met a well-situated family by the name of Cotta. They took an interest in the bright youngster, and kept him in their home during his studies at St. George's school.

While young Luther may not have thought much at that time about a life in the church as a monk or a priest, the church was never far from him. He awoke to the ringing of church bells, and he was taken to church as part of his schooling. His teachers were men who had received religious training. Churches and monasteries, monks, nuns, and priests were everywhere to be seen. Religion in all its forms was all about him. Should trouble ever strike, the solution religion offered was obvious and at hand.

Chapter 3

The Monk

Martin Luther's decision to enter a monastery on St. Alexius Day, 1505, angered his father and shocked his friends. Four years earlier, he had begun to prepare himself to study law, in accordance with his father's wishes. In the spring of 1501, he had entered the University of Erfurt to begin work toward the examinations for the bachelor's and master's degrees, which would qualify him for graduate study in law.

For the B.A., he studied grammar, rhetoric, Aristotelian logic, astronomy, physics, and psychology. He listened to fairly dull and usually predictable lectures based on standard textbooks. He also attended formal public debates between university professors, and participated in public debates with his fellow students. This was a customary and exciting part of university education in Luther's time. It trained students to explain and defend the knowledge which they acquired, and was considered important for every profession, whether it be theology, law, or government.

Luther did all this very well, passing his B.A. examinations in the fall of the next year, the earliest possible time that he could take them. He proceeded immediately to prepare for the M.A. exam, studying mainly the works of Aristotle on science, philosophy, and ethics. He also studied Euclid's geometry and other classical writings. A bachelor of arts was also a teaching assistant, and while studying for his M.A., Luther introduced new students to grammar, rhetoric, and logic, the subjects he had recently learned. In January 1505, at age 21, he passed his M.A. examination, ranking second in a group of seventeen. Later, he remembered the excitement of the graduation exercises, with a torch parade preceding the new masters, and he observed, "There is really no temporal or worldly joy just like it."

A master had the duty to serve the university as an instructor for two years. During this time, one customarily studied in one of the graduate departments: theology, law, or medicine. Having chosen law, he bought expensive legal textbooks and began his studies about May 1505.

What happened next is described in one of the famous "table talks" given by Luther 34 years later: "On July 16 (1539), Alexius Day, Luther said, 'Today is the anniversary of my entry into the monastery at Erfurt.'

And he began to tell the story about his vow. Two days before Alexius Day he had been on a journey on foot near Stotternheim, not far from Erfurt. He was so terrified by a bolt of lightning that he called out in sheer terror, 'St. Anne, help me, and I shall become a monk.' And he continued, 'But God understood my vow as if made in Hebrew. *Anna* means by "grace" and not by law. Later I regretted my vow and my friends tried to dissuade me from keeping it. But I remained steadfast. On the eve of Alexius Day I invited some good friends for a farewell dinner. The next day they took me to the monastery, but when they again hesitated to let me go I told them, today you see me for the last time. They said good-bye with tears. My father was very angry about my vow, but I remained true to my intention. I never thought that I would ever leave the monastery. I had died to the world until God chose a time and confronted me with Sir Tetzel and Dr. Staupitz encouraged me to take a stand against the Pope.' "

It is a strange story. Luther had certainly been exposed to thunderstorms before. Other reasons must have contributed to the decision. At age 21, an intelligent and sensitive young man is likely to ask the question, "What is the meaning of my life?" He had been successful in his studies. He might ask, "Is this all there is to life?" For many religiously inclined young people, the monastery was the place where one might be able to

This 20th-century photograph of Erfurt shows a view of the monastery that Luther entered in 1505. Construction of the Augustinian church was begun in 1131.

live a life pleasing to God and humanity, preparing for an eternity in the presence of almighty God.

If the three basic questions a human being must confront are: "What can I know? What must I do? What may I hope?" (Kant), Luther had gone very far very fast in his quest for knowledge. Life as a monk might help him to find answers to the other questions.

From all we know, he was a most sincere monk. Of the eight monasteries in Erfurt, he had chosen one belonging to the "observing Augustinians," known for the seriousness with which they followed the ancient rules. Seven times a day he went to chapel for prayer. He confessed his sins frequently and went to Mass. Later, he observed: "I was a good monk, and I kept the rule of my order so strictly that I may say that if ever a monk got to heaven by his monkery it was I. All my brothers in the monastery who knew me will bear me out. If I had kept on any longer, I should have killed myself with vigils, prayers, reading, and other work."

Luther did everything expected of him, and was soon accepted as an outstanding member of his community. He was chosen for the priesthood, ordained deacon and priest, and on May 2, 1507, not quite two years after the fateful decision to enter the monastery, he said his first Mass, an event which deeply moved and even terrified him.

His superiors selected him for further study, and he studied theology. This led to his appointment in the fall of 1508 to the faculty of the recently founded University of Wittenberg. He lectured in philosophy and continued his study of theology, receiving a bachelor of Bible degree in 1509. That same year he was recalled to Erfurt, where he continued to study and to teach. From November 1510 to April 1511 he accompanied an older monk to Rome who had to present concerns of the German Augustinians before the international leadership. Neither the beauty of the landscape nor the art of the Holy City impressed him. He returned, still searching for the meaning of life, asking the question, "How can I be sure that God loves me?" The faithful pursuit of the monastic life had not given him the answer.

Professor Bainton has summarized the significance of Luther's stay in the monastery most aptly: "The great revolt against the medieval church arose from a desperate attempt to follow the way by her described. Just as Abraham overcame human sacrifice only through his willingness to lift the sacrificial knife against Isaac; just as Paul was emancipated from Jewish legalism only because as a Hebrew of Hebrews he had sought to fulfill all righteousness, so Luther rebelled out of a more than ordinary devotion."

He saw this revolt as an act of obedience to the God he had tried to serve by becoming a monk.

Chapter 4

The University Professor

One of Luther's most important teachings was his claim that God does not want you to leave your work in the home, on the farm, in the office, the factory, or the school, in order to find salvation in some other, more "religious" place. God can and will save you where you live and work. As economists and sociologists have noted, this teaching has contributed to the development of the so-called Protestant work ethic. It has had a profound influence in the Western world, especially in northern Europe and North America.

Luther's view was largely a description of his own experience. He had tried—without success—to save himself by being a good monk. The harder he tried, the more depressed he became. But in the summer of 1511 he was again assigned by his Erfurt superiors to teach at the University of Wittenberg. There his dean, Johann von Staupitz, who knew him from his previous stint, told the 27-year-old monk to prepare for the doctor of theology degree in order to become a regular professor at the university. This was surprising, because at Erfurt no one under 50 years of age received that degree. Luther protested his youth, his poor health, and the very considerable expense of obtaining the degree, which would be wasted if he should die soon, as he expected. Dean Staupitz told him that it was the decision of the senior members of the monastery that he should seek the degree, and if he were indeed to die soon, Staupitz suggested that God might be able to use doctors of theology in heaven. Luther obeyed. The elector of Saxony, proud of his fledgling university, paid for the expenses of the degree, and Luther became a doctor of theology on Oct. 19, 1512. His assignment at the university was to teach Bible, which he did for the next 34 years.

Doing his job as a teacher of the Bible, preparing his lectures and participating in debates, Luther discovered the gospel. Not while desperately trying to save himself by subjecting himself to the strictest monastic discipline, not by fasting and self-mortification, but while doing his assigned task as teacher of the Bible, he was given the insight that salvation is not a human achievement, but a divine gift. Luther knew the Bible. For years, he read it through once every six months. He compared it to a mighty tree and every word of it to

Luther's discovery that salvation is God's free gift came not through fasting or self-mortification in the monastery, but through his work as a teacher of the Bible.

little twigs, and he claimed that he had knocked on every one of these twigs to discover what they might be able to teach him. People who heard his lectures and debates commented on the fact that the entire Bible seemed always available to him when his position was questioned. It was the study of the Bible which led him to the overwhelming experience that the righteousness through which women and men are saved and become God's children is not their achievement at all. It is a divine gift, awarded by God out of incomprehensible and unmerited grace because of the life, death, and resurrection of Jesus Christ, and accepted by human beings by faith alone. Luther was sure that the Bible teaches this everywhere. This is the gospel, the good news, which constitutes the only treasure entrusted to the church. Everything not related to this gospel of God's grace for Christ's sake is not Christian.

Luther scholars have debated for decades about when exactly it was that Luther came to this insight—precisely when it was that he discovered the gospel. Some give dates as early as 1513 or as late as 1519. Without taking sides in this debate, it is obvious to any reader of Luther's works that between 1513 and 1520 the implications of the gospel as a divine gift became ever clearer to him and were expressed with increasing power.

It took a long time until Luther realized that what he had to say about the gospel on the basis of his study of Scriptures was creating conflict with the established church, which made reconciliation ever more difficult, if not impossible. Luther's comfort in this situation was that he had not raised this issue without a proper call from God. He had been assigned the position of doctor of theology against his own wishes. Thus, the church itself had given him the right and duty to call Christians back to the Holy Scriptures. The church lives by obedience to God's Word. He had been called by God to serve the church as teacher (doctor) of this Word. This was not a matter of personal opinion, or the polite avoidance of controversy. God's cause was at issue. In his Lectures on Romans of 1515-1516, he had said: "Because I hold the public teaching office on apostolic authority it is my duty to identify what is wrong in the church—even among my superiors." When he sent his 95 theses to Archbishop Albrecht of Mainz, he signed the accompanying letter: "Martin Luther, Augustinian, called to be doctor of sacred theology."

Luther discovered the gospel and his responsibility for it not by running away from the world—as he had once tried—but by doing his job as a teacher of Holy Scripture. From this experience, he concluded that all women and men should wait for God not in places of their own choosing, but wherever they had been placed.

Chapter 5

The Indulgence Controversy

The events which made Martin Luther, an obscure theology professor in a shabby little town in Saxony, into a famous reformer had a good deal to do with money.

In the course of his biblical studies, Luther had discovered the truth, "the righteous shall live by his faith" (Heb. 2:4). He thought, quite correctly, as most Christians would claim today, that this was the faith of the one holy, catholic, and apostolic church which had been obscured for him by his foolish endeavor to save himself by his own good works.

Here the matter could have ended, if only a major advertising campaign promoting the sale of indulgences had not been launched in the neighborhood of Wittenberg. It was an effort to raise money to pay the debts of

Albrecht of Hohenzollern, archbishop of Magdeburg, bishop of Halberstadt, and archbishop of Mainz. Since it was against church law that one man should hold more than one such position at a time, he needed a suspension of this law.

The pope had the power to do that, and he was willing to oblige for a price. The situation was further complicated by the fact that Albrecht was only 23 years old, legally too young for such offices, and had no theological training whatsoever. Pope Leo X, a member of the Medici banking family, made all the necessary arrangements. He charged a huge sum, which Albrecht borrowed from the Fugger banking house, and arranged for the repayment by allowing the new multiple archbishop to pay his debts with money raised through the sale of indulgences in Germany.

Professor Bainton has called indulgences "the bingo of the sixteenth century." But the matter was really more serious than that. Most people who play bingo in church do it for entertainment. There may be some greed involved, but none believe that his or her eternal welfare is promoted by playing bingo. Indulgences were different. Whatever they had meant originally, in Luther's time many people believed that they could secure their eternal salvation, or even the liberation of loved ones who had departed this life and were now thought to suffer in the prison of purgatory, by buying letters of indulgence. Whether or not the church taught that indulgences had such power, many people believed

Johannes Tezelius Dominicaner Münch/ mit seinen Römischen Ablaßkram/welchen er im Jahr Christi 1517. in Deutschen landen zu marckt gebracht/wie er in der Kirchen zu Pirn in seinem Vaterland abgemahlet ist.

O ihr deutschen mercket mich recht/
Des heiligen Vaters Papstes Knecht/
Bin ich/vnd br in euch itzt allein/
Zehn tausent vnd neun hundert care in/
Gnad vnd Ablaß von einer Sünd/
Vor euch/ewer Eltern/Weib vnd Kind/
Sol ein jeder gemehret sein
So viel ihr legt ins Kästelein/
So bald der Gülden im Becken klingt/
Im hup die Seel im Himel springt/

Als Bapst Leo der zehend genand/
Nu mehr fast vnmüglich befand/
Das er das Römisch Jubel Jahr
Erlebet/hat er die faule wahr/
Des Ablaßkrams in Deutschenland/
Durch seine Kramknecht ausgesandt/
Dazu sich denn ohn all verdrieß/
Johann Tezel gebrauchen ließ/
Der was itzt kaum dem Hencker entlauffen/
Als er wegen Ehebruchs solt ersauffen/
Wo nicht der from Fürst Friederich/
Seiner sich angenommen sich/
Vnd beim Keyser Maximilian/
Ein gnedigste Fürbit gethan/
Hierbey es aber so nicht blieb/
Aus eim Ehebrecher wurd ein Dieb/
Welch durch vermeint gewalt vnd macht/
Viel Gelds vnd Guts zu weg gebracht/

Als er die blinde Welt bered/
Das er den Himel feil tragen thet/
Wenn man nu Gelt gnug gebe dar/
Hets mit den Menschen kein gefahr/
So bald der Grosch im Kasten klingt/
So bald die Seel in Himel sich schwingt/
Durch diesen Teuffelischen Tande/
Hat er betrogen sein Vaterland/
Biß ihn Gott hat ins Spiel gesehen/
Durch Doctor Luthern seligen/
Welcher ihm seinen Krämertisch/
Gewaltiglich zu Boden stieß/
Daher/Gott lob/biß auff die zeit/
Der Ablaßkram zerstrewet leit/
So bleibet nun Christi verdienst/
Einig allein vnser Gewinß/
Des Tezels Kram vnd Bapsts Betrug/
Findet bey vns kein recht noch fug.

Many people in Luther's time believed that the purchase of saints' relics would secure their salvation or shorten the amount of time their deceased relatives spent in purgatory.

36

it and were willing to spend their hard-earned money for these pieces of paper.

The indulgence craze was promoted by high-pressure salesmen who used clever publicity, advertising jingles, and scare tactics to boost their sales. Bainton quotes one such sales pitch: "Listen to the voices of your dear dead relatives and friends, beseeching you and saying, 'Pity us, pity us. We are in dire torment from which you can redeem us for a pittance.' Do you not wish to? Open your ears. Hear the father saying to his son, the mother to her daughter, 'We bore you, nourished you, brought you up, left you our fortunes, and you are so cruel and hard that now you are not willing for so little to set us free. Will you let us lie here in flames? Will you delay our promised glory?'" The jingle that went with this plea was: "As soon as the coin in the coffer rings, the soul from purgatory springs."

Luther heard about this promotion from his parishioners. He served a parish, listened to confession, and said Mass. The men and women who came to confess told him that, since they had purchased indulgences, they no longer had to worry about their relationship with God. They had not been able to buy these letters in Wittenberg, since Luther's prince, Frederick the Wise of Saxony, had prohibited their sale in his territory. But in those days Germans had only to walk a few miles to be in another state, under different rulers, where indulgences were easily available.

Luther took action against the indulgence sales because he considered them a fraud and a danger to the spiritual welfare of Christians. He wrote *95 Theses*— short sentences which he wanted to debate—to clarify the issue, call the attention of the authorities to these abuses, and, if possible, stop the nonsense. Today scholars argue whether he actually nailed the theses to the door of the castle church. He, himself, never said he did. In any case, they were widely circulated, and caused heated debates everywhere. They opened with the assertion that repentance must be a new attitude toward God and the life God has given us. This new attitude cannot be replaced by paying money. Luther insisted that the pope could not possibly be responsible for the nonsense the indulgence peddlers promoted, for every Christian who is truly sorry for his sins will receive God's forgiveness for Christ's sake, even without letters of indulgence. The pope, no more and no less than any other priest, declares God's forgiveness to those who repent. "Christians should be taught," Luther wrote, "that he who gives to the poor or lends to the needy does better than if he buys indulgences. . . . They should also be taught that a person who sees people in need and passes them by to buy indulgences is not purchasing the indulgence of the pope, but calls down the wrath of God upon himself." If the pope actually knew of the activities of the indulgence peddlers, he would rather see the basilica of St. Peter burned to ashes than that it should be built with the skin, flesh, and bones of his sheep. Luther quoted others who scoffed that if the pope had the power to release people from purgatory, he should do it out of love, and not for money.

Almost everybody who read these theses was impressed. Overnight, Luther had become an important voice people were heeding. Those who needed the money collected through indulgences were worried. Indulgences involved big money, supporting all kinds of good causes: churches, hospitals, universities, even roads and bridges. With his attack against indulgences, Luther had kicked Humpty Dumpty off the wall, and it soon became apparent that neither kings nor popes nor emperors could put him back together again.

Chapter 6

The Great Debates

After Luther had raised the question whether the practice and beliefs of the church of his time, as illustrated by the sale of indulgences, were truly Christian in the light of the gospel, the immediate result was a series of debates. These public confrontations of opposing points of view were the accepted method of establishing the truth in Luther's time. Luther had hoped to solve the question of the validity of indulgences. But it soon became apparent that much more was at issue than these dubious sales. The very nature of the Christian faith appeared to be involved. In April 1518, half a year after the publication of the *95 Theses,* Luther was invited to Heidelberg to present his theological position. As was the custom, one of his students actually presented the theses which Luther had prepared for this occasion, and Luther presided over the disputation. The theses ignored indulgences and attacked the theology which, in Luther's opinion, had made the sale of indulgences possible.

First of all, Luther insisted that the law of God, good and true as it is, cannot make human beings good. Human works, even though they might appear to be splendid, are sins as long as the person performing them is a sinner. Everything a sinner does is sin: "The law works wrath: it kills, curses, makes guilty, judges, and damns everyone who is not in Christ." You are a Christian, not because of your good works, but because you trust Christ, who alone can make you what you ought to be. Furthermore, Luther said, the love of God does not seek for lovable people; rather, God, by loving people, makes the unlovely lovable. Human beings act the other way around. We are always looking for people who are worthy of our love, and constantly complain that our love is not appreciated.

These theses of Luther proved to be quite controversial, for they turned popular religion right on its head. Ask anybody in Luther's time, or ours, and you will discover that most people think of God as a judge —we might even say the "great computer in the sky"— who keeps perfect track of what we are doing and rewards or punishes us according to our record. When people say blithely, "All religions are the same," they refer to this element in all religion which makes God into the referee in the game of life, handing out medals

41

to the winners and reprimanding or penalizing the losers. In Heidelberg in 1518, Luther said that such belief is the opposite of what the gospel of Jesus Christ proclaims. Good works do not make us good, and only good people are able to do good deeds.

Luther himself did not think that this was such a novel discovery. Jesus had frequently said that a good tree bears good fruit and a bad tree evil fruit. People cannot make themselves into good trees by decorating themselves with good fruit. Only God can make a tree good and enable a person to do good works. Not everybody who heard Luther in Heidelberg agreed with him, but some young listeners, like Bucer, Brenz, and Pellican, who later became important leaders of the Reformation, were won over to his cause.

The second important debate took place from June 27 to July 14, 1519, in Leipzig. While Heidelberg had been a meeting of scholars, Leipzig turned out to be quite a theological circus. Originally, the debaters were to be Dr. Johannes Eck of the University of Ingolstadt, and Dr. Andreas Carlstadt, an older colleague of Luther's, who had arranged the disputation. Luther and Philipp Melanchthon, his brilliant young colleague and friend who had joined the Wittenberg faculty, went along for the ride. It was quite a procession. They traveled in horse-drawn wagons. Carlstadt came first, then Luther and Melanchthon. Two hundred Wittenberg students, armed with spears and pikes, jogged alongside

At the Leipzig Disputation of 1519 Luther engaged in debate with Johannes Eck of the University of Ingolstadt.

the wagons to show their loyalty and make sure that nothing happened to their teachers.

The debate started slowly. While Eck was a brilliant debater, Carlstadt was slow and tended to get lost in his learned quotations. Finally, on July 4, Luther got into the act, and things began to happen. The issue was the authority of the leadership of the organized church. Eck insisted that the pope was the head of the church on earth; Luther said Jesus Christ is the only head the church has and needs. (The rule of the pope over the other bishops was not recognized in the ancient church. The Council of Nicea knew nothing of it, and neither did Augustine.)

While Luther's assertions might sound radical to Roman Catholics in our time, they did not appear so to the audience in 1519, 350 years before the declaration of papal infallibility at the First Vatican Council. What appeared shocking to Luther's listeners in Leipzig was his subsequent claim that not only the pope, but even the universal church councils, may err. Indeed, he said, the respected Council of Constance, where John Hus had been burned at the stake as a heretic, had condemned very Christian and evangelical teachings of Hus.

To get Luther to make this admission was a major success for Eck. Now Luther was associated with a Bohemian archheretic who was not only despised for his errors, but also hated for the devastation which his followers had inflicted on Germany after his death.

Heidelberg and Leipzig served to clarify three important issues in Luther's teaching: 1) The distinction between law and gospel. Only the gospel can save—the law condemns all people. 2) All human beings and institutions can and do err. Thus, the reformation of the church is always needed. 3) Jesus Christ is the sole head of the church. Human beings have authority only if they obey Christ and his Word.

Chapter 7

1520

1520 was a crucial year in Luther's life. The pope and his lawyers and theologians in Rome had begun to take him seriously. On June 15, Leo X released an official statement called a bull (because of the *bulla,* the seal affixed to it) condemning 41 teachings of Luther and giving him 60 days to take them back. Should he fail to do so, he would be excommunicated. The pope, known as an avid hunter (people could not kiss his toe, as was the custom, since he was always wearing hunting boots), was staying at his hunting lodge, and there added an introduction to the bull reflecting his obsession with wild animals: "Arise, O Lord, and judge thy cause, a wild boar has invaded thy vineyard."

The publication of this bull resulted in the public burning of many of Luther's books. The predictable

Bulla contra errores
Martini Lutheri
τ sequacium.

The title page of the bull issued by Pope Leo X against Luther. The first sentence of the bull said, "Arise, O Lord, and judge thy cause, a wild boar has invaded thy vineyard."

response of the "wild boar" was a public burning of books of canon law and scholastic theology in Wittenberg. Luther himself threw the papal bull into the fire. Later he wrote, "Since they have burned my books, I burn theirs." These events prove only that paper is combustible.

But it was Luther's use of paper to publish his ideas which made 1520 so important. Three books in particular are of great significance for the Reformation and the development of the Protestant movement. The first book Luther called *An Open Letter to the Christian Nobility*. Addressing the emperor and the political leaders of Germany, he asked them, as baptized Christians, to take part in the reformation of the Christian church. So far, he wrote, this task had been frustrated by three walls which the Papists had built to prevent any reform: 1) The government had no right to pass laws that affected the church. Clergy were exempt from the judgment of lay courts. 2) Only the pope could interpret the Bible. 3) Only the pope could call a universal Christian council to reform the church.

Luther rejected the distinction between laity and clergy. Only Baptism, gospel, and faith make a person a Christian, and laity and clergy have equal access to these divine gifts. "There is really no difference between lay people and priests . . . 'spiritual' and 'temporal' as they call them except that of office and work." Christ does not have two bodies, one "temporal" and another "spiritual." He is one head and has one body. As members of this body, all ought to help each other, and, for the sake of all Christians, it is high time to put the church in order.

The second wall is even more flimsy. The Bible shows that Peter, allegedly the first pope, was corrected by Paul, who understood God's will better. The third wall does not stand either. Peter did not convene the Apostolic Council, and Emperor Constantine, not the pope, called the Council of Nicea. The pope didn't even attend.

Luther submitted a long list of issues which a general council convened by the emperor might consider, from the conspicuous consumption and worldliness of the popes to a basic reorganization of the structures of the church to enable it to serve all human beings, not only church officials. He also argued that the clergy should be free to marry. He reminded his readers that the Bible warns that to forbid people to marry is a doctrine of devils. Luther also listed issues of particular concern to government: schools for boys and girls should be established, high interest rates reduced, and alcohol abuse restrained (since it not only wastes money, but results in "murder, adultery, stealing, irreverence, and all the vices").

Luther's second book dealt with theological issues. He called it *The Babylonian Captivity of the Church*. It advocated the reform of the Mass. Bread and wine should be given to all communicants (at that time, the wine was withheld from the laity). Christ is really pres-

49

ent in the bread and wine, though these physical objects are not changed. The Mass is not a good work, performed by human beings to appease God; rather, it is God's gift to people. Luther also taught that Baptism is God's promise of salvation which must be accepted in faith. He did not believe that other Christian rites like confirmation, marriage, ordination, or unction were sacraments at all: "Hence there are, strictly speaking, but two sacraments in the church of God—Baptism and the Bread; for only in these two do we find both the divinely instituted sign and the promise of forgiveness of sins."

The third book, called *On Christian Freedom,* was very short and quite different. It does not reflect the bitter conflict surrounding its author, but rather describes the Christian faith and life, and especially how life flows from faith. Starting with the paradox, "A Christian is a perfectly free lord of all, subject to none," and "A Christian is a perfectly dutiful servant of all, subject to all," Luther explained the Christian life in the light of the Word of God. Distinguishing between the Word of God and words of God, he insisted, "The Word is the gospel of God concerning his Son, who was made flesh, suffered, rose from the dead, and was glorified through the Spirit who sanctifies." If people trust this Word, they are united with their Lord. Christ takes their sins and gives them his righteousness. The result of this exchange is Christian life, since, while good works do not make a person good, a good person does good works. As God has helped me, I should help my neighbor: "And each should become as it were a Christ to the other."

By 1520, Luther's position had been clearly stated. Men and women are saved *by grace alone*. They lay hold of this grace *by faith alone,* which itself is a gift of God, as demonstrated in infant Baptism. All baptized Christians are priests, called to share in Christ's work of love and service guided *by the Scriptures alone.*

Chapter 8

Worms and Wartburg

Two places besides Wittenberg will be forever associated with Luther: the city of Worms and Wartburg Castle. Worms was the location of the Diet of 1521, a congress of princes and bishops ruling the empire. After complicated negotiations, Luther had been invited to Worms to recant his errors (as his enemies saw it), or to present his views and be refuted or vindicated by Scripture (as his friends assumed).

His appearance at Worms led to a dramatic confrontation between the descendant of peasants and miners—the monk now teaching at a small university in the backwater of European civilization—and the Holy Roman Emperor, who ruled an empire stretching from eastern Europe to southern Italy, and from the Netherlands to Spain and the Americas.

The date was April 17, 1521, the time, 4:00 P.M. For the first time, Emperor Charles laid eyes on the man who was to complicate his rule immeasurably. His immediate reaction was, "That chap will never make a heretic of me."

Asked to acknowledge a stack of books piled on a table before him, Luther answered that they were indeed written by him, and that he had written even more. The questioner continued: "Do you defend all of them or are you willing to reject a part?" This was a perfect opening for Luther to raise doubts about the authenticity of some of his more controversial writings, and draw attention to those writings where he had attacked the money-raising schemes and political machinations of the papacy. On those issues he had wide support at the Diet. Charles, now emperor, had been opposed by the pope when seeking the office. Even now, the pope was conspiring with the Muslim Turks against the emperor. It was a golden opportunity to focus on the questions relevant to the politicians, and play down the theological controversy. But Luther replied: "Because this is a question of faith and the salvation of souls, and because it concerns the divine Word, I might come under Christ's judgment when he said, 'Whoever denies me before men, I also will deny before my Father who is in heaven,' I beseech your imperial majesty for time to think." The strength of Luther's position resided in his unwillingness to play politics. In a

Docto: Martini Luthers offen-
liche Verhör zů Worms jm Reichs tag/
Red/Vnd Widerred Am.17.tag/
Aprilis/Jm jar 1 5 2 1
Beschechen

Copia ainer Missiue/Docto: Martinus Luther nachsei-
nem abschid zů Worms zů rugck an die Churfür-
sten/Fürsten/Vñ stend des Reichs da selbst
verschriben gesamlet hatt.

*At the imperial Diet of Worms Luther refused to retract
any of his writings unless first convinced of his errors by
Scripture and sound reason.*

54

very political meeting, he caught everybody off guard by talking about loyalty to the Word of God.

Reluctantly, he was given another day to think things over. When he appeared on April 18, he made a short speech describing the different kinds of books he had written, and concluded, "Unless I am convinced by the testimony of the Scriptures or by clear reason . . . I am bound to the Scriptures I have quoted and my conscience is captive to the Word of God. I cannot and will not retract anything, since it is neither safe nor right to go against conscience. I cannot do otherwise, here I stand, may God help me. Amen." Scholars have been debating whether Luther actually said "Here I stand," but this is a trivial matter, for whether he said these words or not, he had lived them by standing before the most powerful people of his time and not retreating an inch from his total commitment to the Word of God. When he later taught people to sing "Lord, keep us steadfast in your Word," he knew what this prayer meant.

The emperor, who did not understand German, was not impressed. Luther was allowed to leave Worms, but an edict was issued which called him a "devil in the habit of a monk" and banned him (thus allowing anybody who found him to kill him at sight). On the way from Worms to Wittenberg, Luther disappeared. Many feared he had been killed. The German painter Albrecht Dürer wrote in his diary, "O God, if Luther is dead, who will henceforth explain to us the gospel?"

Actually, he had been kidnapped by masked soldiers of Frederick the Wise, to be hidden at Wartburg Castle to await further developments. In this ancient fortress, separated from his friends, he had time to meditate on his situation. He grew a long black beard, dressed as a knight, and was called Knight George. But he kept on writing. Once some books had arrived from Wittenberg, he continued his commentary on the Magnificat, the song of Mary whom he loved, and whose humility he admired. He wrote biblical commentaries and theological treatises. But his most important work at the Wartburg was translation of the New Testament from the original Greek into German. There had been earlier German translations, but they were based on the Latin translation of Jerome, and, as translations of translations, were fairly unreliable.

Luther's Bible translation is outstanding because he combined theological profundity with eloquence and an uncanny gift for finding the right word in German for the original Greek term. Because his translation of the Bible unified countless dialects into a standard German, Luther has been called the creator of the German language.

He stayed at the Wartburg from May 4, 1521 to March 1, 1522 while the Reformation continued without him. The loneliness and isolation helped him to clarify his own position. Standing at Worms before emperor and empire had been important. Sitting in his room at the Wartburg meditating on the Word of God and translating the Bible proved equally important. The Reformation needed the bold confessor at Worms; it needed the thinker and scholar at the Wartburg as well. Great changes are brought about by thought and action. Because Luther combined the ability to do both in an admirable way, the Reformation succeeded.

Chapter 9

Conflict
and Controversy

Luther reached the peak of his popularity in 1521 as the result of his courageous stand at Worms. Had he died then, the Reformation might have failed, but the reformer would have remained a hero. The German knights, men like Hutten and Sickingen, saw him as a champion of their rights against foreign priests and domestic bankers. The intellectuals considered him an eloquent voice defending education against ignorance and stupidity. The peasants heard a man who advocated Christian freedom for everybody. Religious people with independent views admired him as a sincere advocate of freedom of conscience, and even the persecuted European Jews, expelled from Spain and England, hoped that Luther might support their aspirations.

Indeed, the Jewish hopes seemed to be justified. In

Many German knights, such as Ulrich von Hutten, hoped that Luther would help them in their fight against foreign priests and the economic changes that were threatening their status in society.

59

1523 Luther had written a book, *That Jesus Christ Was Born a Jew*. Here he asserted that Jews had been so badly treated by so-called Christians that, "If I had been a Jew and had seen such dolts and blockheads govern and teach the Christian faith, I would sooner have become a hog than a Christian." He also observed that forbidding Jews to labor and do business like other people was forcing them into usury and thus their participation in this activity was not to be held against them.

But Luther's preoccupation with the gospel soon lost him the support of all those who had hoped to use him and his cause for their own purposes. The knights engaged in fruitless battles with the princes which Luther neither encouraged nor understood, and soon faded forever from the scene. The intellectuals like Erasmus found Luther too preoccupied with faith and not sufficiently concerned with learning. Luther's theology stressed the utter dependence of men and women on God and left no room for Erasmus' liberal notions concerning the freedom of human beings in their relationship to God. Some were also offended by Luther's admittedly coarse language.

The peasants were at first encouraged by Luther's sympathy for their cause. Commenting on their demands, he had written to the rulers, "You do nothing but cheat and rob the people so that you may lead a life of luxury and extravagance." But when the peasants took the law into their own hands and revolted against their rulers, Luther sided with the princes, because, to his horror, the peasants were calling their revolution the work of God. Luther considered this idolatry, and encouraged the rulers to "stab, smite, and slay." When the peasants were quickly defeated, Luther had lost much support among the common people.

Luther never changed his position in regard to freedom of conscience. When Thomas Müntzer challenged his interpretation of the gospel, Luther advised the elector of Saxony not to interfere in the theological controversy. "Let the ideas contend with each other," he wrote. But Müntzer was not satisfied with theological arguments; he joined the peasant revolution. Then Luther urged his prince to use force. From then on, his confidence that any of his opponents were willing to contend with words alone was gone. He saw them all as revolutionaries who must be held in check by force of arms. He was sure that all the people he called "Anabaptists" and "Enthusiasts" were using theology as a pretense for armed revolution. They were trying to establish the kingdom of God on earth with fire and sword. He believed what he had written in the *Small Catechism* while explaining the meaning of the prayer "Thy kingdom come": "To be sure, the kingdom of God comes of itself, without our prayer, but we pray in this petition that it may also come to us." For human beings to attempt to usher in God's kingdom was blasphemous pride.

Most regrettable and tragic was Luther's attitude

toward the Jewish people. At first, he was considered a friend of the Jews. He had studied Hebrew and insisted that without this language there can be no understanding of the Scriptures; for the New Testament, though written in Greek, is full of Hebrew expressions. "It is rightly said," he wrote, "the Hebrews drink from the fountains; the Greeks from the streams, and the Latins from the pools." Luther spent most of his professional life explaining the Old Testament.

Shortly after the publication of his first book dealing with the Christian attitude toward the Jews, Jewish scholars visited him and tried to engage him in serious discussion. They were, of course, unwilling to accept his Christ-centered interpretation of the Old Testament. But since this is the basis for Luther's understanding of Scripture, their attitude seemed to him stubborn and evil.

Still another development poisoned the relationship. He heard from various sources that Jews were using his writings attacking the established church to call into question the validity of the gospel and to tell people that the Messiah had not come and that they should wait with the Jews for the arrival of the true Messiah. There were, indeed, Jews who hoped that Luther's work might be a sign of the impending arrival of the long-awaited Savior.

The indefensible violence of Luther's outbursts against the Jews in his later years can be best explained, though not excused, by the fact that the Jews had questioned him at the most sensitive point in his theology. Luther explained everything in the Bible from Genesis to Revelation by means of the life, death, and resurrection of Jesus the Christ. When this foundation was attacked, he lashed out with incredible fury. In his conflict with the Jews, the great theologian of the cross revealed his triumphalist Achilles' heel.

Luther, who had discovered the gospel in the quiet of the monastery, had to defend it in the midst of constant acrimonious controversy. This fact shaped his language and style. To us, the form of his arguments seems frequently crude and offensive; the intention, however, is always clear: "Lord, keep us steadfast in your Word!"

Chapter 10

Word and Sacrament

In the midst of controversy and under attack by the conservative supporters of the papacy as well as the radical foes of all tradition, Luther claimed that the Christian life depends entirely on God's gifts of grace. The two gifts which create and constantly renew God's people are Word and sacrament.

Luther's hymns show the importance of God's Word for his faith. In "A Mighty Fortress Is Our God" (LBW 229; © 1978 LBW), he sings, "God's Word forever shall abide, No thanks to foes, who fear it." And, similarly, he prays: "Lord, keep us steadfast in your Word" (LBW 230).

For Luther, the Word is first of all the Lord Jesus Christ himself. As far as Luther was concerned, long before there was a Bible, the eternal Christ, God's

A portion of the altarpiece by Lucas Cranach in the city church in Wittenberg. The full scene shows the congregation gathered at the far left as Luther points to the crucified Christ in the center of the painting.

Word, created the heavens and the earth. This very same Word guided the saints and sages of the Old Testament. On Christmas this Word was born as a human baby. Luther sang: "Once did the skies before Thee bow; A Virgin's arms contain Thee now" (CSB 18).

Not only is Christ the second person of the Trinity, he is God's Word. Wherever and whenever he is proclaimed to men and women, they hear and meet the Word of God. Preaching is for Luther the most important activity of the church because it means that here people are exposed to the living Word of God. Thus he can describe the work of the preacher in the most glowing terms: "Each day through him many souls are taught and converted, baptized and brought to Christ and saved and redeemed from sin, death, hell, and the devil." When we hear God's Word proclaimed, we meet the living God today, because the Holy Spirit can make this Word so alive to us that we become Christ's disciples today just like those women and men who walked on earth with him 2000 years ago.

But the Holy Scriptures, the 66 books from Genesis to Revelation, are also the Word of God. The Bible is for Luther the manger in which we find Christ, the swaddling clothes in which he is wrapped. This means that we must take care to worship the Christ and not the manger or the swaddling-clothes. For Luther, this implied that there is a proper way of reading and interpreting the Bible. It must always be read with Christ in mind. Only then can it be properly understood.

Christ is the key to the Scriptures. "What does not teach Christ is not apostolic," he wrote, "even though St. Peter or Paul taught it; again, what preaches Christ would be apostolic, even though Judas, Annas, Pilate, and Herod did it." Apostolicity has nothing to do with particular human beings; it is faithfulness to Christ. He applied this notion to the Old Testament as well as to the New.

During most of his life as a professor, Luther lectured on the Old Testament. Genesis was one of his favorite books. But he read it with Christ in mind and it became for him the proclamation of the gospel. While Luther made a very clear distinction between God's law and gospel, this is not the same as the distinction between Old and New Testament. Both Old and New Testament proclaim law and gospel. The law is God's demand. It can be found in the Ten Commandments in Exodus as well as in Galatians, where Paul warns, "Do not be deceived; God is not mocked, for whatever a man sows, that he will also reap" (6:7). But for Luther, the gospel is proclaimed both in the election of Abraham and Moses and in the death and resurrection of Jesus.

There are many legitimate ways of reading the Bible; it can be read as ancient literature or Jewish history, for example. Luther read it only one way: as the story of salvation through Jesus Christ, the descendant of David, the child of Mary, the Son of God.

But Luther knew still another way in which God bestows grace: through "visible words"—the sacraments. While the number of sacraments was not very important to him (for a while he thought there were three: Baptism, the Lord's Supper, and Confession), he settled on two because he thought that they alone were instituted by Jesus during his earthly ministry. Marriage, for example, though a divine order, was established long before Jesus' birth to aid women and men in their life together.

Baptism was, for Luther, ordination into the priesthood of all believers. All Christians are called to serve the world as ambassadors of Christ. But in their service to each other and to the world as instruments of God's love, they need constant strengthening through the presence of Christ and the forgiveness of sins. Therefore the Lord has instituted the Lord's Supper to empower Christians for their service.

Luther believed that Christ was really present in the bread and wine of the Lord's Supper. Because of his promise, "This is my body" and "This is my blood," these ordinary elements of food become the body and blood of Christ for all who believe in his Word. This does not apply only for those who consider themselves "worthy." Luther was adamant that even the unworthy would receive the true body and blood of Christ in the Lord's Supper. Thus, regardless of our merits, Christ is present for us and with us, and in the sacrament of the altar we receive a foretaste of the heavenly feast that awaits all who trust in Christ.

The Christian church can function in many different ways. For some, it is a social club where like-minded people gather. William Lazareth has called such a church "a Teutonic alumni association." For some, it is a remnant of the faith of our fathers and mothers which we no longer share, a museum one rarely visits. Still others consider the church a holy club, where those who are no longer sinners meet to celebrate their achievements and gloat over the outsiders on their way to hell. For Luther, it was the communion of saved sinners, where God's Word is proclaimed and the sacraments are administered. Word and sacrament alone create and sustain the church.

Chapter 11

Faith Active in Love

Most people who know something about Luther consider him a major voice in the Christian church. Even those who do not like him will usually admit that he was an original thinker who deeply affected the Christian church and the Western world. But it is also part of the conventional wisdom that, while Luther spoke eloquently about the Christian faith, he cared less about the Christian life; while his concern for theology was powerful, his interest in ethics was weak. No doubt his abusive remarks about popes and peasants, Anabaptists and Jews have contributed to this reputation.

Yet nothing could be further from the truth. Luther became involved in the Reformation because the indulgence sales tended to undermine the moral standards of his parishioners. He spoke out because these sales were demoralizing and deceiving simple people.

Indeed, those who have completed confirmation instruction in a Lutheran church know, from studying Luther's *Small Catechism,* about the profound ethical concern expressed in his explanations of the Ten Commandments. "You shall not kill" became for Luther the counsel not to cause neighbors any harm, but rather to help and befriend them in every necessity of life. Not to steal means also to assist your neighbors to improve and protect their incomes and property. Not to bear false witness meant, for Luther, to apologize for your neighbors when they are under attack, to speak well of them before their enemies, and to interpret charitably all that they do.

The Christian faith must show itself in a Christian life. As a good tree bears good fruit, faith is active in love. Luther claimed that if people live Christian lives only for the rewards they hope to gain from God, they are bound to neglect the true interests of their neighbors in this world in order to accumulate greater rewards for themselves in heaven. For example, if giving alms to the poor results in rewards for the generous givers, they are not motivated to abolish poverty, since doing so would also do away with an opportunity to gain further merits. Thus begging is encouraged, because it gives beggars the opportunity to demonstrate humility, while generous almsgivers accumulate merits through acts of charity.

71

Luther claimed that since Christians are saved by God's grace, they do not have to worry about obtaining merits in order to qualify for heaven. They are now free to concern themselves with the true interests of the sick, the poor, the lonely, and the sad. God's forgiveness of sins frees human beings *from* preoccupation with their own interests and *for* service and care of those people who really need help. It is much better to abolish poverty than to give alms to the poor.

For Luther, human beings are channels of God's love, instruments through which God helps those in need. Luther insisted that this happens in a variety of ways. God raises children through mothers and fathers; educates the ignorant through teachers; keeps human beings from destroying each other through police and judges; heals through nurses and physicians; and uses pastors and missionaries to make the Word known throughout the world.

Faith active in love means to accept our responsibility as God's agents in the world, to live our lives, whatever our occupation, as an opportunity to show God's love. Of course, in trying to do this we might become discouraged. Just as we rarely show our gratitude to God, so the people we help tend to be ungrateful to us. We soon discover that the world does not change as easily as we had hoped, and our best intentions frequently produce unsatisfactory results. Luther knew all this very well and reminded his readers that the power that undergirds a truly humane human life is the forgive-

A 1529 portrait of Luther by Cranach. This oil-on-wood painting now hangs in St. Anne's church in Augsburg.

ness of sins. God's forgiveness enables us to live as free men and women looking toward the future, not obsessed by the past. This same power of forgiveness which makes possible our life in the presence of God should also enable us to forgive those who sin against us.

Students of Luther's theology have observed that the gospel of the forgiveness of sins is at the very center of his thought. But it describes not only how God deals with human beings; forgiveness is the divine power that enables parents to deal with children and children with parents, wives with husbands and husbands with wives. It is the power that makes it possible to live with an impossible boss or an equally impossible employee. It is God's power poured into human beings to enable them to live a Christian life. For Luther, the Christian life is real and possible, not as a human achievement, but as a divine gift. He was convinced that God was willing to bestow this gift on all, regardless of their merits or qualifications, if they were only willing to accept it.

Chapter 12

The Legacy

There are many reasons for remembering Martin Luther. His work changed the Western Christian church fundamentally and irreversibly. Some of the changes, such as the use of the language of the people in worship and the singing of hymns by the congregation, have been universally adopted. Indeed, some of the descendants of people who resisted Luther fiercely in the 16th century are singing his hymns joyfully in the 20th. Many of his ideas have proven fruitful not only for theologians, but for historians, philosophers, and psychologists.

He affected the language of the German people permanently and profoundly. His translation of the Bible did as much for the German language as the King James Version did for English. But, above all, his courage at Worms in the face of church and empire so impressed Christians hundreds of years later that black parents in America were naming their sons after him to honor and perpetuate this courage.

The effect on the worldwide church is probably the most important element of Luther's legacy. The medieval monk from a small village in East Germany eventually became a symbol for the entire Christian community. What does he symbolize today?

He symbolizes, first of all, the importance of reformation for the Christian movement. Reformation must not be something that happened once upon a time hundreds of years ago and is forever completed and that one can now take for granted. It must be a permanent element in the life of the Christian church; it has to be taken seriously and be implemented by every generation. Only a church that is willing to be reformed today can honestly claim Luther as its reformer.

Much of what he said at the beginning of the 16th century has to be said in new ways at the end of the 20th. Luther changed Christian worship in his time so that people would be able to understand it and participate. A Lutheran church where worship has become a spectator sport is not properly celebrating Luther's birthday. He made theology something to be debated and appreciated by politicians and farmers, artists and artisans. When the church makes theology a secret science understandable only to an intellectual elite, it has betrayed the heritage of Luther.

For Luther, the very life and substance of the church
depended on the Word of God in all its fullness:
Christ, preaching, the sacraments, and the Scriptures.
Pictured is a portion of the title page to the 1541 edition of
Luther's Bible.

Second, Luther knew that the church depends entirely on God's Word. He wrote: "The entire life and substance of the church is the Word of God." This Word, he said, is Jesus Christ, it is the living proclamation of Christ to all people in Word and sacrament, and it is the Holy Scriptures. Without the Word in this inclusive and many-sided sense, the church is nothing but a social club, a museum, or a concert hall. To celebrate Luther's birthday meaningfully is to remember or rediscover what makes the Christian church the people of God: trust in Jesus Christ, the Word of God. We could not celebrate Luther's birthday better than by beginning a serious study of the Bible in all our churches. What ultimately reformed the church was not Luther, but the Word of God Luther was explaining in his sermons, commentaries, pamphlets, and letters.

Third, Luther knew that a saint is a sinner saved by grace through faith in Jesus Christ. The church is holy because Christ, the head of the church, is holy even though the members of the body remain sinners in constant need of forgiveness and new strength. Thus Luther wanted an inclusive church where the sick are healed, the poor fed, the sad comforted, the ignorant taught, and sinners saved. A church that is socially, radically, intellectually, or even morally exclusive does not take Luther very seriously. If at the birthday party for Martin Luther only "our kind of people" are welcome, we have not understood Luther. He claimed that the church of his time erred by not accepting "Greeks, Bohemians, and Russians" as members of the same body. One of his objections to the Catholic church of his time was that it was not catholic enough; it had excluded too many people.

The legacy of Luther lives most faithfully wherever God's Word is proclaimed regardless of race or social class, nationality or sex. Luther would be grateful to God to hear people sing his "A Mighty Fortress Is Our God" in Telegu, Zulu, Swahili, Chinese, Slovak, and Hungarian—not because he wrote the hymn, but because it proclaims:

> God's Word forever shall abide,
> No thanks to foes, who fear it;
> For God himself fights by our side
> With weapons of the Spirit.
> Were they to take our house,
> Goods, honor, child, or spouse,
> Though life be wrenched away,
> They cannot win the day.
> The kingdom's ours forever.
> LBW 229; © 1978 LBW

49, 384